A SUMMER NIGHT'S DREAM

Borgo Press Books Edited & Translated by FRANK J. MORLOCK

Anna Karenina: A Play in Five Acts, by Edmond Guiraud, from Leo Tolstoy
Anthony: A Play in Five Acts, by Alexandre Dumas, Père
The Children of Captain Grant: A Play in Five Acts, by Jules Verne and Adolphe d'Ennery
Crime and Punishment: A Play in Three Acts, by Frank J. Morlock, from Fyodor Dostoyevsky
Don Quixote: A Play in Three Acts, by Victorien Sardou, from Miguel de Cervantes
The Dream of a Summer Night: A Fantasy Play in Three Acts, by Paul Meurice
Falstaff: A Play in Four Acts, by William Shakespeare, John Dennis, William Kendrick, and Frank J. Morlock
The Idiot: A Play in Three Acts, by Frank J. Morlock, from Fyodor Dostoyevsky
Jesus of Nazareth: A Play in Three Acts, by Paul Demasy
The Jew of Venice: A Play in Five Acts, by Ferdinand Dugué
Joan of Arc: A Play in Five Acts, by Charles Desnoyer
The Lily of the Valley: A Play in Five Acts, by Théodore Barrière and Arthur de Beauplan, from Honoré de Balzac
Lord Byron in Venice: A Play in Three Acts, by Jacques Ancelot
Louis XIV and the Affair of the Poisons: A Play in Five Acts, by Victorien Sardou
The Man Who Saw the Devil: A Play in Two Acts, by Gaston Leroux
Mathias Sandorf: A Play in Three Acts, by Jules Verne and William Busnach
Michael Strogoff: A Play in Five Acts, by Jules Verne and Adolphe d'Ennery
Les Misérables: A Play in Two Acts, by Victor Hugo, Paul Meurice, and Charles Victor Hugo
The Mysteries of Paris: A Play in Five Acts, by Eugène Sue and Prosper Dinaux
Ninety-Three: A Play in Four Acts, by Victor Hugo and Paul Meurice
Notes from the Underground: A Play in Two Acts, by Frank J. Morlock, from Fyodor Dostoyevsky
Outrageous Women: Lady MacBeth and Other French Plays, edited by Frank J. Morlock
Peau de Chagrin: A Play in Five Acts, by Louis Judicis, from Honoré de Balzac
A Raw Youth: A Play in Five Acts, by Frank J. Morlock, from Fyodor Dostoyevsky
Richard Darlington: A Play in Three Acts, by Alexandre Dumas, Père
The San Felice: A Play in Five Acts, by Maurice Drack, from Alexander Dumas, Père
Saul and David: A Play in Five Acts, by Voltaire
Shylock, the Merchant of Venice: A Play in Three Acts, by Alfred de Vigny
Socrates: A Play in Three Acts, by Voltaire
The Stendhal Hamlet Scenarios and Other Shakespearean Shorts from the French, edited by Frank J. Morlock
A Summer Night's Dream: A Play in Three Acts, by Joseph-Bernard Rosier and Adolphe de Leuwen
Urbain Grandier and the Devils of Loudon: A Play in Four Acts, by Alexandre Dumas, Père
The Voyage Through the Impossible: A Play in Three Acts, by Jules Verne and Adolphe d'Ennery
The Whites and the Blues: A Play in Five Acts, by Alexandre Dumas, Père
William Shakespeare: A Play in Six Acts, by Ferdinand Dugué

A SUMMER NIGHT'S DREAM

A PLAY IN THREE ACTS

by

Joseph-Bernard Rosier & Adolphe de Leuwen

Translated and Adapted by Frank J. Morlock

THE BORGO PRESS

An Imprint of Wildside Press LLC

MMX

Copyright © 2005, 2010 by Frank J. Morlock

All rights reserved. No part of this book may be reproduced without the expressed written consent of the author. Professionals are warned that this material, being fully protected under the copyright laws of the United States of America, and all other countries of the Berne and Universal Copyright Convention, is subject to a royalty. All rights, including all forms of performance now existing or later invented, but not limited to professional, amateur, recording, motion picture, recitation, public reading, radio, television broadcasting, DVD, and Role Playing Games, and all rights of translation into foreign languages, are expressly reserved. Particular emphasis is placed on the question of readings, and all uses of these plays by educational institutions, permission for which must be secured in advance from the author's publisher, Wildside Press, 9710 Traville Gateway Dr. #234, Rockville, MD 20850 (phone 301-762-1305).

www.wildsidebooks.com

FIRST WILDSIDE EDITION

CONTENTS

Cast of Characters 7

Act I: The Mermaid Tavern 9

Act II: The Park at Richmond 85

Act III: The Palace of White Hall 120

DEDICATION

TO

MY SON,

MILES STANTON MORLOCK,

WITH LOVE

CAST OF CHARACTERS

William Shakespeare

Falstaff, Commander of the Guards at the Royal Park at Richmond

Lord Latimer

Jeremy, a tavern keeper

An Usher

An Actor

Jarvis A game-warden (mute)

Elizabeth, Queen of England

Olivia

Nelly (Jeremy's niece)

Actors and Actresses, Courtiers and Ladies of the Court.
Game Wardens, Waiters and Serving Girls
in the Tavern, Kitchen Crew, etc.

ACT I

The Mermaid Tavern

The Mermaid Tavern in London. Entry door at the back; to the right an opening on the banks of the Thames. To the left, a stairway leading to a vast banquet hall. Side doors, rich dressers, armoires. On an armoire at the right, a huge a goblet, bottles; to the left, near a carved wooden bench near a table. Large arm chair near the audience.

CHORUS:

Come on, kids, no laziness!
Our guests will soon be here!
Hurry up, prepare everything.
We must serve zealously!

JEREMY: (to Nelly)

Our best wines?

NELLY:

Are drawn—all sparkling crystal.

JEREMY:

And the roasts?

NELLY:

They are shining on the spit.

JEREMY: (with enthusiasm)

Royal feast.

CHORUS:

Come on, kids, no laziness!
Our guests will soon be here!
Hurry up, prepare everything.
We must serve zealously!

(The entry door in the back on the right opens, and a ship with men debarking can be seen.)

JEREMY:

Why, who's coming here?
Could it already be a guest?
Yes, it's Sir John Falstaff, joyous epicure

Of the feast being prepared. Honor. let's do honor
To Sir John, this noble lord

ALL:

All honor, honor, let's render honor
To Sir John, the noble lord.

FALSTAFF:

Let's go, let's all prepare
Let's sing,
Let nothing hold us back
Let's drink
The greatest shame
Here!
To the one who insists
Thanks!
And Cupid! And Bacchus!
Yes, drink to,
And feast
These gods that we love.

CHORUS:

Companions, sing, etc.

FALSTAFF:

Falstaff is very friendly,
My word!

He's always dining
At the king's.
For melancholy
He's absent.
Companions, come on sing
And Cupid, and Bacchus
Yes, let's drink to
And feast
These gods that we love.

CHORUS:

Companions, let's sing, etc.

JEREMY: (approaching Falstaff with a bottle and a huge goblet, respectfully presenting the goblet to Falstaff)

Excellent, Sir John, deign to take
Your glass.

(pouring)

And taste this wine
I'm going to serve festively,
As ordered by you.

FALSTAFF: (after having swallowed, expansively)

It's fine!
And on my soul it's spreading
Warmth

And joy.
Here I am in very good humor!

CHORUS:

Ah! What an honor!
Ah! What a joy.
Milord
Is in good humor!

FALSTAFF:

Look—now that I'm inspecting
All the settings for our supper
For us, nothing's too expensive is suspected.
I am not the one to be fooled.

JEREMY:

It's not you they want to cheat
You are going to see.

(speaking through an opening communicating with the kitchen)

Cooks, roaster, look smart!
Get prepared!

SUBTERRANEAN CHORUS:

Cooks, roasters, look smart!

Let's get prepared!

JEREMY:

The feast hall is open—
Let's hurry up!

VOICES:

The feast hall is open—
Let's all hurry up!

FALSTAFF: (taking the horn)

John Falstaff, your wise leader
He is here!

VOICES:

John Falstaff—Our wise leader
He is here.

FALSTAFF:

Under arms he makes all appear
Before him.

VOICES:

Under arms he makes all appear
Before him!

FALSTAFF: (to Jeremy)

Think that this evening you have the singular honor
Of receiving Shakespeare and his friends.
This banquet must be worthy of the great poet.
Or your ovens shall be forever cursed
By me!

GENERAL CHORUS:

Cooks, roaster, look smart!
Let's prepare!
The feast hall is open
Let's all hurry there!
John Falstaff our wise leader
Is here!
Under arms he makes all appear
Before him.

(Great culinary parade. The Roasters carry in a huge plate covered with venison, and in the midst of it— The wine waiters have baskets filled with bottles. Several pastry cooks carry a pyramid of pastries on a litter.)

FALSTAFF:

What a sight! What an august spectacle!
Halt!— Let me taste.

(all obey as commanded and stop.)

FALSTAFF: (after having smelled the plates)

This banquet
Appears perfect to me!
The bouquet
Of this wine pleases me!
This—is truly flirtatious.
All is well done!
All is complete!
What a picture! Beautiful weapons
Yes, here they are the true soldiers!
With them, the charmed soul—
One could steal victory on the battlefield.

(Falstaff sits majestically in a huge armchair as all parade before him.)

JEREMY:

Come, with these little delectables
We'll load the table—

FALSTAFF AND CHORUS:

What a picture! Beautiful army!
Yes, here all are true soldiers
With them, the soul charmed
One could steal victory on the battlefield.

(The tavern waiters hoist up the armchair on which Falstaff is seated to their shoulders; they bear him in triumph into the banquet hall. The door at the back opens. Lightning, claps of thunder. Two masked women rush into the tavern.)

DUO:

What horrors! What fright!

ELIZABETH:

Calm down! Calm down!

OLIVIA:

What fright!
I see them.
I think they are following us.

ELIZABETH:

They've lost our tracks.
Appease your terror!

OLIVIA:

Their remarks, their threats
Are making me die of fear.
And this storm
And this uproar—
And these lightning bolts
Splitting the air—!

TOGETHER:

Madame, ah! How reckless
Night is exposing itself so!

ELIZABETH:

I think we've found
A safe shelter in these parts.

(taking off her mask)

OLIVIA:

But where are we?

ELIZABETH:

I don't know exactly.

OLIVIA:

Ah, Madame, frightful night!
Listen—again it seems to me
They're looking for us, pursuing us

OLIVIA:

Madame, how reckless!
See how the night exposes us!

ELIZABETH: (laughing with assurance)

I think we've found
A safe shelter hereabouts.

OLIVIA:

Why, you are able to laugh! It's delirium!
What, you're able to laugh!

ELIZABETH:

Your fright
Is a cruel martyr to fear.
To banish it, sing with me!
Imitate me!

(singing)

King Richard said to his soldiers,
"Courage!
It's by singing one braves the storms of battle!
Ah, in these campaigns
Let's sing my friends
Of our mountains.
Cherished refrain.
Girl
So sweet
Fulfill my hope
Near the brightly shining fire
Come sit down

Tonight
What a sweet
Rendezvous.
But let's hide
From all jealous eyes!"

OLIVIA:

To sing here—it's delirium
Ah! Stop, mercy!

ELIZABETH: (laughing)

Why?
Fear is a cruel martyr
To banish it, sing with me!
King Richard found glory
On his path.
And as the Saracens fled before him,
Victory.
But far from the fatherland
That his heart loved.
His voice became tender
Always repeating—
"Sweet girl," etc.

OLIVIA:

Your courageous soul
Is too adventurous!
What an unlucky night

That I don't follow till tomorrow.
To brave the dark night
And run adventures.
Ah, as for me, I swear it.
It's painfully cruel!

ELIZABETH:

Yes, I am courageous,
I have an adventurous soul!
And I feel myself happy
When at last I am free!
I swear I'll prefer
Braving the dark night
To run adventures
Like a true paladin!

(speaking)

Yes, once again, my child,
Calm down.

OLIVIA:

Ah! What imprudence to have wanted
To be present incognito
At the performance of this work
By Shakespeare.

ELIZABETH:

Isn't it natural that this young
Poet interests me? His life, all the
Details of which, I've had told to me
Has, up to now, been a series of
Bizarre accidents, of contrasts, and
Tonight, I was vainly hoping
That he would be called back
That he would appear on stage,
After his resounding success.
I've never seen him, and I would
Have been curious to know if the
Nobility of his features corresponded
To the elevation of his mind.
For one day he will be the first poet
In England.

OLIVIA:

But from what they say: what morals.
What scandalous conduct.

ELIZABETH:

Ah! Why doesn't he have close
To him a powerful friendship to
Snatch him from this abyss where
His high intelligence is in danger
Of perishing. It seems to me that
We are still there, behind

The curtain of our little box!
The two of us gathered there, moved,
Attentive! What delightful moments
We spent, didn't we Olivia?

OLIVIA: (distractedly)

Yes, yes, delightful, madame.

ELIZABETH: (noticing and smiling at Olivia's preoccupations)

Come on, you are acting from complaisance. And indeed, I recall, why my gaze never left the stage, where my mind was ravished, my ear enchanted. Your eyes were there. On a box facing us, fixed on a noble cavalier.

OLIVIA: (sighing)

Yes, I saw him. But as for him, he wasn't looking at me.

ELIZABETH: (smiling)

Well, it's not you I pity, it's him.

OLIVIA:

Yet, still, if we'd been able to go back in peacefully, but no—outside we found a shocking storm and a tumultuous crowd, separated from two gentlemen accompanying us, pursued by drunken sailors, troubled, losing our heads, we finally fell—

ELIZABETH: (looking around her)

In a place quite sheltered, quite calm, where no one is seen and no one is heard, from what it appears.

OLIVIA: (frightened)

Yes, this was a refuge!

ELIZABETH: (laughing)

From brigands, right? No, it's quite simply a tavern, a rich tavern which forgot to lock its doors after curfew.

OLIVIA: (terrified)

A tavern!

ELIZABETH: (smiling)

My God, calm down, scaredy-cat! Aren't you with me?

OLIVIA:

Yes, madame, I'm a scaredy-cat, timid, that's my nature, like yours is courageous and determined.

(enthusiastically) But if your life, if your honor ran some danger, I would have enough strength to rush to your side, and to sacrifice my honor and my life to you.

ELIZABETH:

Noble child! Yes, I know your devoted friendship, but in these circumstances you won't have to give me proof of it. And then look, Olivia, see…. (pointing to parchments)

OLIVIA:

Oh, the seals of the High Sheriff!

ELIZABETH:

With which my prudence is always armed, and I would merely have to trace a few words above the signature to obtain obedience, to get help for us, without revealing who we are. But we won't have need of them.

(listening) Because the storm is calming; within an hour we will have returned to London or gone to Richmond, and the end of the night will seem sweet to us after the torment troubling its beginning.

OLIVIA:

Yes, but tomorrow, tomorrow when we are asked for—

ELIZABETH: (proudly)

Who would dare question me?

OLIVIA:

You, madame, no one. But as for me, he will dare, he will dare.

ELIZABETH:

Your noble cavalier? What! Is he jealous to this degree?

OLIVIA: (pointing to the flowers that she wears in her girdle)

Yes, madame, and to complete the misfortune, this morning he offered me this bouquet saying: "Tonight, after you wear them for a long while, give me one flower to perfume my night and enchant my dreams."

ELIZABETH:

Well, tomorrow you'll give him the whole thing. And now that the tempest has dissipated, let us pursue our lost trail.

OLIVIA:

Let's not wait for the night to be more advanced. I have a horrible fright here.

ELIZABETH:

Well, let's be going, Olivia, and under God's protection.

(they replace their masks and start to leave)

FALSTAFF: (leaving the banquet hall and stopping at the rear)

Two masked women!

OLIVIA: (aside)

Heavens!

ELIZABETH: (low to Olivia, rapidly)

Falstaff.

OLIVIA:

The keeper-general of Richmond.

ELIZABETH:

Fear nothing. Here we are in a land of acquaintances and even obedience.

FALSTAFF: (grabbing them)

Where are you running to, my beauties?
Under these shading masks?
My sweet turtle-doves,
What are you seeking here?

ELIZABETH: (with irony)

Past master of love,
Can't you guess?

FALSTAFF (conceitedly)

Yes, I ought to recognize
Such seductive allures!
The adventure is divine,
Forgive me, but I believe
That my heart knows you
And that you seek—

ELIZABETH:

Well?

FALSTAFF:

Well—it's me you're looking for!

OLIVIA: (to Elizabeth)

Ah! What impertinence!
To speak to us like that!

ELIZABETH: (laughing)

Ah, what conceit
Let's amuse ourselves with him.

FALSTAFF: (fatuously)

Yes, I am confident
That it's me you're looking for!

(a silence)

FALSTAFF:

What's to prevent you?
It's easy to understand
You've seen me,
I've pleased you,
Your little hearts surrendered.
That's understood,
That's agreed.

ELIZABETH: (laughing)

Ha! Ha! Ha! Who'd have thought it?
This fine gallant! He pleased us,
Our hearts surrendered to him.
That's understood,
That's agreed.

OLIVIA: (likewise)

Ha! Ha! Ha! Who would have thought it, eh?

ELIZABETH: (with irony)

You imagine you know how to please us?

FALSTAFF: (fatuously)

I flatter myself as to that.

(gesturing to Elizabeth to remove her mask)

No more mystification!

ELIZABETH:

Hold on! We'll agree about it.

OLIVIA: (excitedly)

What are you saying?

ELIZABETH (to Falstaff)

And we will love you
If, my dear master, you can guess
Who it is we are?

FALSTAFF:

By Jove! Is it possible to mistake you?

(to Elizabeth) This coquettish and pretty foot,

(to Olivia) This dazzling hair do—

(to Elizabeth) Robert, the innkeeper, you're his cousin Bess!

ELIZABETH: (disdainfully)

Better than that—

FALSTAFF: (to Olivia)

And you are Alison
The daughter of a Brewer

ELIZABETH:

Get out!
A tavern keeper, a Brewer, ah! Get out!
Mount, my dear, a step.

OLIVIA:

Mount, my dear, a step.

FALSTAFF:

I've got it! Lovable pair, you are
The daughters of our constable
Maggie, and Jenny—

ELIZABETH:

Better than that!

OLIVIA:

Get out!

ELIZABETH:

A constable, get out!
Mount, my dear, a step.

OLIVIA:

Mount, my dear, a step

FALSTAFF: (to Elizabeth)

Got it! Got it! You are Arabella
The wife of the Sheriff

(to Olivia) And you my all beautiful
Her servant Nelly.

OLIVIA:

Better than that, get out!

ELIZABETH:

Climb up a step!

OLIVIA:

Climb up a step!

FALSTAFF:

We'll climb up a step further.
This time no more errors

(he bows to the ground)

Before you, I abase myself

(to Elizabeth) You are the Queen!

(to Olivia) And you, a princess.

OLIVIA: (aside, terrified)

Ah, Great God!

ELIZABETH: (aside)

What's he say?

FALSTAFF:

Princess.

(laughing) —of the stage! In these parts tonight
At the prepared banquet, you'll come and be seated.

ELIZABETH: (getting control of herself)

He scared me—

OLIVIA: (likewise)

I'm still trembling—

FALSTAFF: (fatuously)

I've divined it.
How they adore me!
Your little heart surrendered
You saw me
I pleased you
It's understood,
It's agreed.

ELIZABETH: (laughing and mocking herself)

Ha! Ha! Ha! Who would have thought it?
This fine gallant, he pleased us—
To him, our hearts surrendered.
It's understood,

It's agreed.

OLIVIA: (likewise)

Ha! Ha! Ha! Who would have thought it?
This fine gallant, he pleased us—
To him, our hearts surrendered.
It's understood,
It's agreed.

ELIZABETH: (jesting about Falstaff)

Handsome cavalier. You are not clever.

FALSTAFF:

I've guessed.

ELIZABETH:

You've guessed nothing!

OLIVIA:

Recognize us, ha! That's not easy.
But as for you, we know you quite well.

FALSTAFF: (fatuously)

By Jove, in London town
My name is familiar to all the beauties.

ELIZABETH:

The name itself, is little, but as for me, I'll answer for it
I know all your characteristics.

FALSTAFF:

What? You know all my characteristics?

ELIZABETH:

Your characteristics and your inclinations!
I know how to recognize you,
You are, my master,
In love most treacherous,
Like a true miscreant.
Pursuing
Each day you contract new debts
Under a false identity
All your boasting,
Your courage,
Your rodomontade,
Are nothing but false airs!
I wager you will be cited
From one age to the next
Like an assembly
Of all the misfits

FALSTAFF:

Ah, damnation! I'm enraged.

Can anyone treat me like this?
Must beauty's favorite
Be outraged?

ELIZABETH AND OLIVIA: (laughing, aside)

Ah, how furious he is
That we dare to treat him like this.
I'm laughing at his fury
Ah, let's make fun of him.

FALSTAFF:

Come, come, my charmers,
Don't be cruel. You came here
For me. That's evident. Besides,
Now I recognize you.

(to Elizabeth) You, Giddy, merry, and wanton.

(to Olivia) You, Timid, finicky, tremulous.
And me, lovable, witty
And handsome chevalier.
Thus

(pointing to Olivia) The mistress.

(pointing to Elizabeth) The servant

(pointing to himself) And the gallant—
Unfortunately, I am quite busy

This evening, an artists'
Convention. Preparation of a
Banquet celebrating Shakespeare.

ELIZABETH: (excitedly)

Shakespeare? You know him?

FALSTAFF: (fatuously)

You ask if Falstaff knows Shakespeare?
Ask rather if Shakespeare knows Falstaff!
Ask rather if the Moon knows the Sun.
And if the Sun knows the—
Yes, I know Shakespeare!
I, who, myself cannot resist him
Glass in hand! I, who he cannot do without.
I, who he dubbed his shadow.
The huge shadow of the great Shakespeare.

ELIZABETH: (aside)

Oh! How I'd like to see him!

(aloud) And this banquet is to take place?

FALSTAFF:

In a few moments.

ELIZABETH:

Here?

FALSTAFF:

Here!

(to Olivia) But my word, you are very seductive, and I'll make them bad company. It shall not be said that you have launched me for nothing to the Mermaid Tavern.

ELIZABETH:

What do you mean?

FALSTAFF:

I renounce the banquet. True, without me they won't drink much, laugh much, or sing much, or break much. But who cares? I shall lead you—

OLIVIA:

Where to?

FALSTAFF: (mysteriously)

To my house in Richmond.
At the edge of the Royal Park.

OLIVIA:

Oh, in that case we'll be saved!

ELIZABETH: (aside)

To miss such a fine opportunity to convince my self, by myself.

FALSTAFF: (to Olivia and Elizabeth)

Well? What do you say about that?
We will improvise a nice little supper;
For in my capacity as game-warden-general of Richmond
I eat the Queen's best venison.

(to Elizabeth) The Queen doesn't count them.

ELIZABETH: (standing right in front of him)

Ah!

FALSTAFF:

Yes.

(to Olivia)

You'll taste the finest fruits of the royal reserve.
I only allow the Queen the second best.

(to Elizabeth, laughing) The Queen never suspects a thing.

ELIZABETH:

Ah!

FALSTAFF:

Yes!

ELIZABETH: (aside)

The royal residence is in need of major reforms.

FALSTAFF:

Well? Do you accept?

OLIVIA: (whispering to Elizabeth)

We must. At Richmond we'll be in greater safety than here.

(aloud)

We accept!

FALSTAFF: (aside)

I was sure of it.
I'll get them both.

ELIZABETH: (to Olivia)

Come, since we must.

FALSTAFF: (offering his arm to Olivia)

I am the happiest of men.

(musing, looking to the rear)

What do I see? Torches!
Too late. It's too late.
It's Shakespeare with his guests.

ELIZABETH: (joyfully)

Shakespeare!

FALSTAFF:

You mustn't be seen. Actors, gentlemen, a bad lot Shakespeare in the lead.

OLIVIA:

What to do?

FALSTAFF: (pointing to the side door on the left)

Go in there—in that room; once the banquet begins I'll come to get you and we'll leave.

OLIVIA: (fearful)

Here they come.

FALSTAFF:

Go! Not a moment to lose!

(they enter the door, Falstaff locks it after them.)

CHORUS:

Let's sing his glory,
And his brilliant success!
So that his memory, Friends, will live forever!
Honor to the poet!
Ah, let him be fêted
At this fest.
Let each prepare
And let all repeat
Some gay refrain.

SHAKESPEARE: (to an actor)

For tonight, changing madness:
Come, come, my dear Hamlet.
While savoring wine
You'll be clinking glasses with Macbeth.

(to another actor)

And you, my sensitive Ophelia
Fill this glass to the brim.
Thanks to you, Macbeth shall forget
His remorse and his spouse.

CHORUS (refrain)

Let's sing his glory
And his brilliant success, etc

LATIMER: (aside, sadly)

How much I envy
Their folly and frivolity!
Ah! For me, tonight,
It's goodbye sweet hope.
Olivia, I must never see you again!

SHAKESPEARE:

Now, where then is Falstaff?
Falstaff! Will you answer?

FALSTAFF: (near the door the two women went in)

Present!

SHAKESPEARE: (laughing)

He was there! I didn't see him at all.

FALSTAFF:

My word!
P'raps I'm becoming
Invisible.

SHAKESPEARE: (laughing)

A bit like the Tower of London!

(singing)

Children, how beautiful the night!
Let's celebrate, yes, and keep celebrating
Life, faithful friendship
And inconstant love.
No more misery here!
My heart is young again.
Heaven, at the bottom of a glass
Disposes us to forgetfulness.
Drives away cares.
Flee boredom.
Day and night, my friends.

CHORUS:

Drive away cares, etc.

JEREMY: (entering with solemnity)

Master William is served!

SHAKESPEARE:

What a joyous messenger.
Let's hasten to render ourselves to his call.
We must never make either the public or our supper wait!
Friends, pleasure and folly
Are offering us their hands.
Quickly, to table where we'll join together
Let's rush, rush to the feast.

CHORUS:

Friends, pleasure and folly, etc.

CHORUS:

Ah, let our joyous shouts
Hurl themselves towards the heavens!
Let's sing, sing in chorus:
Friend dear to our hearts
Yes, he'll live forever.
William, they will celebrate you
On stage forever—
Both your glory and success.

SHAKESPEARE:

So long as my heart beats,
It will always love
Those who forever
Made my glory and success.

(All except Shakespeare go into the banquet hall. Falstaff makes a face as if to follow, then mysteriously retires behind the masked women's door. Shakespeare, as he is about to enter the banquet after the others, notices Latimer, who's absorbed in his thoughts. Shakespeare stops.)

SHAKESPEARE: (aside)

Well, what's my noble friend Lord Latimer doing?

LATIMER: (to himself)

Where can she be at this hour?

SHAKESPEARE: (loudly)

Milord!

LATIMER: (still absorbed)

Why'd she break her word to me tonight?

SHAKESPEARE:

My gentleman.

LATIMER:

Oh! My jealousy!

SHAKESPEARE: (coming downstage)

What are you thinking of, milord?

LATIMER: (coming to himself)

Ah! It's you, my friend?

SHAKESPEARE:

The banquet has begun. Already joyous toasts are being made; generous wines sparkle in cups, frivolity shines in every face. It's the prologue to the feast, and each of us has a role. Come!

LATIMER:

Shakespeare, I will not go.

SHAKESPEARE:

You're jesting, Latimer. You won't insult me by missing a feast that's being given for me, at which you promised to be present.

LATIMER:

It's true, but I was counting, I was hoping before coming here, to find the one I love at a rendezvous we regularly have.

SHAKESPEARE: (smiling)

And you didn't find her?

LATIMER:

No. And I am asking myself why.

SHAKESPEARE:

Why? A thing that is changeable, changes.

LATIMER:

Change? Her!

SHAKESPEARE:

They're all alike!
And it's useless to deny it.
You are jealous.

LATIMER:

Me!

SHAKESPEARE:

You! And here's the way not to be. So as not to be jealous, and not to feel jealousy, one must—

LATIMER: (excitedly)

One must—

SHAKESPEARE: (smiling)

One must
Love all women.

LATIMER:

All?

SHAKESPEARE:

Just all the pretty ones, you understand.

LATIMER:

What! William, once your heart has dreamt—

SHAKESPEARE:

After the heart has dreamt it must wake up. And once awake, it must observe that the lady of its dreams, and the lady of reality are two different ladies.

LATIMER:

What! You imagine that my heart can love several times.

SHAKESPEARE:

As oft as it meets lovable creatures.

LATIMER:

Why, that's treason, infidelity.

SHAKESPEARE:

Calm down, friend. Look, do you betray your love for mountain highlands because you also love mysterious vales? Are you unfaithful to a heaven fully resplendent with stars because you also love the sea's foaming waves? Trust me, this inconstancy in the heart of man is but apparent. 'Tis but a homage rendered to that singular, sovereign, immutable beauty from which spreads all the changing and mobile beauties of this changing, mobile universe.

LATIMER:

William, a secret bitterness can alone cause you to speak thus. Perhaps you were deceived once.

SHAKESPEARE:

Consider: instead of once say always, and you'll have it just right.

FALSTAFF: (appearing, aside)

They're not at the banquet.

(he disappears again)

LATIMER:

No, I cannot remain here besieged by suspicions. I am going.

SHAKESPEARE:

Stay, I won't let you leave in a state that solitude can only worsen. Come to my party.

LATIMER:

No, my friend. And besides, what a figure I would cut there,
My preoccupations would contrast—

SHAKESPEARE:

Exactly. Contrast. That's what's needed. That's what gives relief to all. See this picture here. Skeptical Shakespeare, joyous one day, melancholic the next, on his right side, the tender, silent Latimer, and on his left, the gay, the fat, the rotund, the chubby, the boastful buffoon Falstaff.

FALSTAFF: (reappearing)

They're still there.

SHAKESPEARE: (to Latimer)

So come, friend, come make your contrast.

(in a different tone)

You shall be the gentle color amidst hot, noisy, or vigorous colors. You will be the soft note in the midst of this noisy concert, the azure cut-out that makes shadowy clouds emerge. Come Latimer, come, they're waiting for you.

(he moves away from Latimer)

LATIMER:

Well, go!

SHAKESPEARE:

And you don't want the consolations of friendship?

LATIMER:

No!

SHAKESPEARE:

Friendship will forget you.

LATIMER:

Let it forget me.

SHAKESPEARE: (near the banquet hall)

You don't want to be distracted from your jealousy?

LATIMER:

No!

SHAKESPEARE:

It will gnaw at you.

LATIMER:

Let it gnaw.

SHAKESPEARE:

You don't want to come to kill time?

LATIMER:

No!

SHAKESPEARE:

Time will kill you.

VOICES: (noises of clinking glasses)

William! William! William!

CHORUS: (from the banquet hall)

Clink, clink, my gay colleagues.
Clink, clink, bid pain g'bye!
Clink, clink, clink over our glasses.
Clink, clink, straight till dawn!

(Shakespeare leaves)

LATIMER: (alone)

Olivia! Olivia!

(singing)

Her image is so precious
It follows me every where, every where.
Away from her, nothing can please me.
My poor heart languishes!
Yes, her presence is the day that lights me.
Alas, her absence is dark night.
It's dark night.
While I dream endlessly

Of the hope which lights us
Tonight, the ingrate forsakes me.
Tonight, she flees me.
No more happiness.
All is changed to sadness.
Alas, her absence is dark night.
It's dark night.

CHORUS:

Clink, clink, etc.

(Latimer reaches the back of the stage)

FALSTAFF: (entering mysteriously)

I no longer see anyone.

(at the door)

Come, come on.

(Latimer, about to leave, turns back and stops. The two women appear)

Now you can remove your masks that you've so obstinately kept on.

(they place their fingers over his mouth in a sign of discretion)

Not yet! Well so be it. Only at my place; but let's hurry; the moment is propitious.

(taking the arms of the two women)

Latimer!

OLIVIA: (aside. Very upset, she removes the bouquet she is wearing on her girdle)

Latimer!

FALSTAFF:

Thanks.

(thinking she wants to give it to him, he takes it and places it under his vest.)

She's mad about me!

(Olivia, overwhelmed with emotion collapses in a chair)

LATIMER: (coming forward)

Ah! My God! That lady is close to fainting. Her mask is bothering her. She must be allowed to breathe.

(going to place his hand on her neck. She shows signs she is better.)

FALSTAFF: (to Olivia)

Feeling better?

(affirmative gesture by Olivia)

That's better—and we can leave.

LATIMER: (watching Olivia emotionally)

Leave? What can you be thinking of in her weakened condition?

FALSTAFF:
It's necessary!

LATIMER:

Well, at this advanced hour of the night, two cavaliers are better than one to protect these ladies.

FALSTAFF:

I will supply it.

(in a whisper to Latimer)

And since I must tell you everything, I'm taking these ladies to my house in Richmond.

LATIMER:

Ah!

(aside then effacing himself)

Falstaff's mistresses.

FALSTAFF: (low to the two women)

Finally we are rid of him.

OLIVIA:

Oh! I thought I was going to die.

(Shakespeare enters half drunk, pursuing Nelly)

NELLY:

William Shakespeare, leave me alone.

ELIZABETH: (turning, aside)

Shakespeare.

SHAKESPEARE:

I tell you I need Falstaff!
Find me Falstaff, bring me Falstaff.

NELLY:

Well, there he is, your Falstaff.

SHAKESPEARE:

With Latimer and two women. So it's a foursome!

(to Latimer)

Hypocrite!

LATIMER:

William!

SHAKESPEARE: (to the two women)

My beauties of the night,
I must present you to our friends.

FALSTAFF:

These ladies are withdrawing; 'tis I who accompany them.

SHAKESPEARE:

Not at all! Your place is
Where I am. Aren't you my
Shadow, Sir John?

FALSTAFF:

Yes, but tonight—

SHAKESPEARE:

Tonight, no one shall leave.

OLIVIA: (in a whisper to Shakespeare)

Oh, I entreat you.

ELIZABETH: (with authority)

And as for me, I order you.

SHAKESPEARE: (laughing)

You order! I alone, I order here and the proof is that I wish everyone to remain until dawn, and everyone shall stay.

(he locks the entry door and takes the key)

OLIVIA: (aside)

O heaven!

LATIMER:

William!

SHAKESPEARE:

Everyone!

FALSTAFF:

All the same—

SHAKESPEARE:

Yes, my shadow. I order you to shut up and go join the others.

(to Latimer) And you, my noble friend, I want you to divert yourself from your languor. You shall not leave. And if I must, at need, I shall bar your passage sword in hand.

(drawing his sword)

I am prepared.

LATIMER:

Intoxication has made him crazy.

(aloud) Place your sword back in its scabbard, William; you are frightening these ladies. I will stay, I will go to the banquet.

SHAKESPEARE:

Right-o!

OLIVIA: (whispering to Elizabeth)

What's going to become of us?

ELIZABETH: (low to Olivia)

Don't be afraid.

NELLY: (wanting to withdraw)

As for me, William—

SHAKESPEARE: (pointing to Nelly's room)

As for you, you are going to take care of this lady—(pointing to Elizabeth)—who demands your attention.

FALSTAFF: (next to Elizabeth, in a rapid whisper)

Here's the key to my house in Richmond. Try to leave quickly with your companion; I will await you there!

LATIMER: (aside, looking at Olivia)

Oh! No, this resemblance is a chimera.

ELIZABETH:

In that room—

SHAKESPEARE:

Near me—

ELIZABETH:

Near you!

SHAKESPEARE:

I wish it!

ELIZABETH: (after thinking about it)

Well, I wish it, too.

SHAKESPEARE: (angrily)

What! Sir John Falstaff,
You are still here?
You are not at the banquet?

FALSTAFF:

I'm becoming inattentive.

(going into the banquet hall)

SHAKESPEARE: (to Latimer)

And you, my noble friend, they are waiting for you.

(Latimer follows Falstaff)

SHAKESPEARE:

Now for the two of us, my beauty, and first of all, you are going to remove your mask.

ELIZABETH:

I intend to keep it.

SHAKESPEARE:

In that case, you are not pretty.

ELIZABETH:

I don't know.

SHAKESPEARE:

You don't know? Then you are modest to be envied, or coquettish to please, or so ugly as to frighten.

ELIZABETH:

What's it to you?

SHAKESPEARE:

What d'you mean, what's it to me? I cannot love you with confidence—

ELIZABETH:

But I don't wish you to love me.

SHAKESPEARE:

Can you prevent me from it? In any case, I insist on knowing if you are pretty.... (coming forward) And will you, nill you

ELIZABETH: (fiercely, stopping him with a gesture)

If you touch my mask, it's your death warrant.

SHAKESPEARE: (with growing astonishment)

My death warrant! Ah, really! So you have the mortal glance of a basilisk in your eyes or a dagger in your belt?

ELIZABETH:

I have what it takes to chastise the boldness of man cowardly enough to do violence to a woman.

SHAKESPEARE:

Now this is becoming curious! Ah, indeed, why in that case what were you doing to come into this tavern?

ELIZABETH:

Chance; an accident led me here! And this locked door which detains me, but, in addition, I was willingly remaining from interest, and because of the pity you inspire in me.

SHAKESPEARE:

From pity? Now this is becoming more and more tantalizing! But do you actually know to whom you are speaking?

ELIZABETH:

I know all the details of your life.

SHAKESPEARE:

Well! I have no such pretension; I've forgotten many things.

ELIZABETH:

Your name is William Shakespeare. Your birthplace, Stratford, in Warwickshire.

SHAKESPEARE:

Yes, and I recall having, in my first childhood, kept flocks in vast solitudes, on mountainsides, amidst majestic silences of nature, alone at night, under heaven's stars. Those nights were the most dream filled, the most fertile, perhaps, and assuredly, the most beautiful in my life.

ELIZABETH:

At eighteen you married a woman of twenty-six.

SHAKESPEARE: (sighing)

Oh! I'll not forget that detail.

ELIZABETH:

Two years later you lost your wife.

SHAKESPEARE:

The gods impose on us the duty of recalling their blessings.

(smiling)

That's one I'll not forget.

ELIZABETH:

After that you led a vagabond life.

SHAKESPEARE:

True enough!

ELIZABETH:

Poor and ill, you came to London where you became a prompter, then an actor, then an author.

SHAKESPEARE:

So who are you to know my past so well?

ELIZABETH:

Would you like to me to tell you your future in brief?

SHAKESPEARE:

Go ahead!

(going to a vat and pouring himself a drink)

ELIZABETH:

William Shakespeare, as your fame increased, your character declined, and each day you degrade your God-given genius.

SHAKESPEARE: (drinking)

Because, barely at the beginning of my career, I needed to forget, to distract myself from the sad realities of my life.

ELIZABETH:

And don't you have your glory? Can't you have a pure love in your heart?

SHAKESPEARE:

Glory? Love? Vanity and chimeras? Do you know what this glory of yours costs me? And at what price can I sell it? It costs me long sleepless vigils, weaknesses of mind and heart, and I am only able to sell it for some gold coins falling from the hands of my audience: the workers and drunks of Blackfriars.

ELIZABETH:

Perhaps our Queen Elizabeth, along with her protection might give you nobler spectators, and if your behavior was more worthy, if instead of wallowing in your gross amours, you had near you a dear and respected spouse—?

SHAKESPEARE:

My first marriage didn't succeed well enough for me to

risk a second.

ELIZABETH:

All women are the same?

SHAKESPEARE:

Yes, like all gloves, like all friends, women cheat, glory disappoints, friends deceive— Only one thing alone in this world gives what it promises—

ELIZABETH:

What's that?

SHAKESPEARE: (pointing to the bottle)

This here.

(drinking)

ELIZABETH:

Enough, Shakespeare, enough, I entreat you.
Already your eyes darken, your steps shake—

SHAKESPEARE:

Well, listen, tonight I need intoxication, profound intoxication. Take off your mask. You must be beautiful. Let me intoxicate myself with your beauty, and I will stop intoxicating myself with this liquor.

ELIZABETH:

Impossible.

SHAKESPEARE:

You're going to keep your mask on?

ELIZABETH:

I'm going to keep it on!

SHAKESPEARE:

In that case, I'm keeping my bottle.

(singing)

In the bottom of my cup, I find
An intoxicating illusion.
A very transitory passion
That banishes sorrow!
Yes, thanks to my bottle
To its vermilion liqueur
My soul awakens
In an enchanting world.
Reason leaves me
Only pain and sadness!

From intoxication
I demand dreams of happiness.
Let's drink without stopping.
Sweet intoxication
Bring me dreams of happiness.

ELIZABETH:

William! Mercy!

SHAKESPEARE:

Oh! Hold on! There's still time. For despite myself and through that mask, the rapid flashes of your gaze dazzle and trouble me. I beg you let that mask fall, and let the charm of your eyes, battle, and wrest from a brutish intoxication the dregs of my vanishing reason.

(looking fixedly at Elizabeth, who hesitates)

Well?

(Elizabeth makes a gesture of refusal)

No?

(singing)

Come on, let's drink without pausing.
Let a profound intoxication
Reign in the place of a mistress

Over my days and my nights.
Let's drink! Let's drink!
O sweet intoxication
Dance in my heart.
Dreams of happiness
Come hither
Drink up!

(spoken)

Ah!

(as he drinks he staggers and falls on his back)

ELIZABETH: (removing her mask and looking at Shakespeare with sorrow)

There he lies, this genius,
This creative mind
Extinguishing itself in an orgy.
What a sight for my heart.

SHAKESPEARE: (drunkenly)

All that reason gives me
Is pain and sadness
Sweet intoxication, give me
Dreams of happiness.

ELIZABETH: (singing)

It breaks my heart to see him like this!
This poet of such beautiful flights.
But he's going to be the laughingstock
Of the grossest bumpkins.
He's betraying his glory.
At least let his crime be hidden.
Ah! Let's shelter this great man from insult,
Like a mutilated masterpiece.

(covering him with her cloak, considering)

But that's not enough for me, or for England! I won't have it:
That a noble mind, heedless of honor,
That this nation should be proud of
Should expire in its first bloom.

(she pulls a writ in blank from her pocket)

Yes, I hope I will succeed,
Then, I'll be his guardian angel.

(hearing a noise, she places her mask back on, and withdraws into Olivia's room, and observes.)

CHORUS: (of Actors)

Friends, a fine feast!
Long live, long live our poet!

A Summer Night's Dream * 75

FALSTAFF (drunk, pursuing Jeremy)

Come on then, innkeeper from hell!
We must be served instantly.
Wine is lacking at our table.
My glass is empty and must be filled.

JEREMY:

Be more reasonable, Sir John.
You've had enough.

FALSTAFF:

Rogue!
You are refusing us.

ALL: (threatening Jeremy)

Wretch!

FALSTAFF:

Let's smash everything in his house.

LATIMER: (rushing in)

Hey! You're losing your minds.

JEREMY:

Gentlemen, be more reasonable, will you—

LATIMER:

Gentlemen, become more reasonable

FALSTAFF:

Since he refuses us wine,
Let's toss the place in the Thames.
Furniture, vessels, no favor.
Him, too, so he can take a bath.

ALL:

In the Thames,
In the Thames.

(The actors chase him to the rear)

JEREMY: (to Latimer)

Prevent them!

LATIMER:

All effort would be vain!

(The guests try to open the door that Shakespeare locked;

unable to do so they bash it in.)

JEREMY:

O heaven!

ALL:

Vessels, furniture, no favor, etc.

CHORUS: (outside)

This is shocking
This is abominable
To make such a noise
In London at midnight.

JEREMY: (tearfully)

Good God, it's the Constable
Who is bringing
The Watch.

ALL:

The Constable.

FALSTAFF:

To the Devil, to the Devil
With the Constable.

JEREMY:

If he sees everybody at my place
At this hour, breaking the law,
I'll be put in the stocks.

(to Latimer)

Mercy, I beg you.
Get 'em out of here.

LATIMER: (to Falstaff)

Let's leave.

FALSTAFF:

No, indeed, my word

(pointing to Jeremy)

Not until this ragamuffin
Pours into my cup
A bottle of Madeira.

ALL (to Jeremy)

Come on, come on, fill my cup!

JEREMY:

And after that you'll all leave?

FALSTAFF:

I promise.

(Jeremy goes to open a cupboard from which he takes some bottles, Elizabeth, with Nelly, has reappeared observing everything. Nelly at a signal from Elizabeth places a letter at the bottom of a large cup that Falstaff has just taken from a dresser.)

ELIZABETH: (aside)

I've just accomplished my plans.

(Elizabeth goes back into the room.)

JEREMY: (returning with bottles, to Falstaff)

Hurry!

FALSTAFF: (extending his cup)

Pour, go on.

(noticing the letter)

What's this? What's it mean?

A letter in my cup?

(fatuously)

Yet another Venus
Wanting to snatch me from Bacchus.

(unfolding the letter)

Let's read!

(struck by surprise)

Heavens!

LATIMER:

What's wrong with you?

FALSTAFF: (trembling, to himself)

It's worth my life if I do not obey.

LATIMER: (coming forward)

This writing? This letter?

FALSTAFF: (recoiling)

Milord, Milord, it's a secret.

(aside, reading the letter with terror, and revealing the bench where Shakespeare lies.)

Him, Shakespeare
To carry him, and without saying anything
To the Palace at Richmond.
By order of the Sheriff.

(to guests)

Quick, quick—we must leave.

(going to the door and making his boatman come forward)

JEREMY: (who's observed him)

The Watch is coming
Leave silently

(making a sign to his waiters)

Put out the lights. That's fine!
They won't see a thing.

(Everyone puts lights out. The stage is dark)

CHORUS OF GUESTS:

Come on, the time's come
We promised
To leave this dwelling.

Let's go, my friends.

FALSTAFF: (returning on stage with four boatmen)

Ah! What extreme worry
Makes me shiver.
But this very moment,
I must obey.

LATIMER: (aside)

Ah. Drive from my soul
The suspicion that pursues me.
Pure love, holy flame,
Olivia, forever unite us!

(Falstaff points out the dozing Shakespeare to his four boatmen)

ELIZABETH: (who's made Olivia come out of her room)

It's time, my dear
We are going to leave.
My plan, I trust
Will be able to succeed.

CHORUS:

Come on, it's time
We promised
To leave this dwelling

Let's go my friends.

(They head out the door at the back as the four boatmen pick up the body of Shakespeare.)

ELIZABETH: (watching them, with joy)

Fine! Fine!

OLIVIA: (to Elizabeth)

What mystery?

ELIZABETH: (whispering)

They are going to obey me.
And for you, my dear,
All will be clarified.

CHORUS OF GUESTS:

Come on, now's the time.
We promised to leave this dwelling.
Let's go, my friends.

(The guests leave. Elizabeth and Olivia escape mysteriously, and the curtain falls as Falstaff and his four men prepare to carry off Shakespeare's body.)

CURTAIN

ACT II

The Park at Richmond

The Thames in the background. To the left a gothic pavilion with a door on the side reached by a few steps.

AT RISE, Night with the moon beginning to shine. A bark can be seen slowly crossing the Thames at the back. In the bark, Falstaff and two boatman, and Shakespeare still sleeping wrapped in his cloak.

Two Game Wardens enter simultaneously from different sides and give calls with their horns. Other horns respond in the distance. The Moon is veiled by clouds.

CHORUS OF FORESTERS:

Guards of the Queen
Over this fine domain
From near to far
We watch with care.
In this pasture

No more poaching
We shall be the terror
Of all marauders.
Hares so timid
Deer so fast
Have no fear
You will have mercy
And you, superb bucks.
In the tall grass
Browse in peace;
We are looking out for you.

FALSTAFF: (to a Warden entering with him)

Jarvis, come on, my comrade
Follow my steps
Don't leave me
Because you are trembling with fear,
And fear makes you ill.

(aside, trembling)

And myself, I agree.
During this dark night,
Ah! Great God! What an adventure!

(aloud)

Jarvis, my friend
Don't tremble like that.
Can you know terror

When your leader is with you?

ALL:

Can you know terror
When your leader is with you?

FALSTAFF: (to the Guards who surround him)

And now, courageous companions,
Attention! Keep the password
You are to surround this mysterious woods,
Forbid all the audacious
From approaching this place at night.

CHORUS:

By our gracious leader
Each of us is made worthy.
Faithful to our orders
No one will approach these parts.

FALSTAFF:

Place yourselves at distance around this forest.
And if I have need of strong hands
At the sound of this horn, all respond.
And fly towards me in a group.

GUARDS:

Agreed!
It's understood.

FALSTAFF: (looking about with fright)

Ah! How black the night.
Jarvis, come on, courage
I am keeping you with me for the fact is notable,
Far from your leader you might be frightened.

(aside, trembling)

Ah, despite my entourage
This mysterious trip
This writing
All come to trouble my mind.
Terror is seizing me!

CHORUS:

Guards of the Queen
Over this fine domain
Near and far
We watch with care!

(The Game Wardens all disperse in different directions)

FALSTAFF: (heading towards the right. Calling Jarvis, who he thinks is still there)

Jarvis! Will you come to me, Jarvis!

LATIMER: (entering from the other side and recognizing Falstaff's voice)

Falstaff!

FALSTAFF: (hearing Latimer's step, going to him thinking he's talking to Jarvis.)

Ah, there you are on the side
Stay with me, my lad.
Never leave me, you'll experience less fear.
I don't know where my head is
Nor even if I have a head.
The fumes of wine,
The emotion of this night
I need to chat with you
Heart to heart.

(letting himself collapse on Latimer's shoulder)

LATIMER: (pushing him away)

What's wrong with you, Sir John Falstaff?

FALSTAFF: (terrified)

Huh? Lord Latimer!
Great God! What's going on for you to be in the Park at Richmond? I've just set guards at all the gates.

LATIMER:

I've been hiding here for the last hour.

FALSTAFF:

Hiding! Profanation! But leave! Hasten! No one must approach the enclosure. I have strict orders and if you were surprised here—

LATIMER:

Me?

FALSTAFF:

Leave forthwith!

LATIMER:

I shall not leave. In a word, what you've told me confirms my suspicions.

FALSTAFF:

What word, milord?

LATIMER:

You said: "If you are surprised here…." I have been particularly designated for your surveillance?

FALSTAFF:

You, like everybody else.
Best go away, mercy!

LATIMER:

No, not before you answer my questions, Sir John.

FALSTAFF:

Speak fast, then—and be careful to speak low, for I am trembling.

LATIMER:

Those masked women who were at the Mermaid Tavern this evening. I had them followed from a distance. They took this direction. They are here, right?

FALSTAFF:

Those women! God! You remind me of it! How impatient they must be!

LATIMER: (urgently)

Those women, those women.
Who are they?
I mean to know. I must know
For despite myself a horrible suspicion pursues me.

FALSTAFF:

Milord, I already told you at the Mermaid, those women are my victims. One of them is especially mad for your humble servant.

LATIMER:

You swear it?

FALSTAFF:

I swear it.

LATIMER:

On what you hold most dear in this world?

FALSTAFF:

Yes. On my head!

(gesture by Latimer to leave.)

(Falstaff begins singing fatuously)

And should you need a final proof
Of the tender love intoxicating her heart
Have a look at this bouquet.

LATIMER: (returning)

A bouquet!

FALSTAFF:

'Tis, I trust
A pledge, an enchanting indication
That I am a happy conquistador.

LATIMER: (trying to identify the flowers)

This bouquet—

FALSTAFF:

Jasmin matched with roses
Behold this ribbon used to bind them.

LATIMER: (enraged)

This bouquet, wretch!!!

FALSTAFF:

What's wrong with you?

LATIMER: (snatching the bouquet from him)

It's mine.

FALSTAFF:

It's mine! Return it.
What sort of folly is this?

LATIMER:

I take you to be the secret agent of some infamous intrigue.

FALSTAFF:

Me? Falstaff?

LATIMER:

You, Falstaff. Admit this bouquet
Is not for you. You're lying. It's a signal
An infernal mystery.

(singing)

This perjury,
This insult.
Yes, I swear it,
You are going to admit it
By your silence.
You will answer to me
For this offense.

FALSTAFF: (speechless)

Why, what perjury?
Why, what insult?
I swear to you
Alas, I'm unaware!
What dementia!
There can be no vengeance
For this nonexistent offense.

LATIMER: (disdainfully)

These flowers for you? Why that's impossible.

FALSTAFF:

I answer to you.

LATIMER:

Shut up! Shut up!

FALSTAFF:

She's sensible of my merit.
You cannot have too much confidence in me.
By his appearance,
His elegance,
And his valor
Falstaff seduces!
For him, our most
Constant beauties,
Even the most rebellious
Lose their heads.

LATIMER:

You will maintain this, wretch!

FALSTAFF:

Yes, my master,
I maintain that the tender object
Who sacrificed this fine bouquet to me
Is burning to see me appear
At a clandestine rendezvous.

LATIMER:

A rendezvous—with you?

FALSTAFF:

A rendezvous—with me!

LATIMER:

Where's that? Reply, double traitor!

FALSTAFF: (pretending discretion)

Oh, pardon! Oh, pardon.

LATIMER (threatening him)

Answer! Answer!

FALSTAFF:

Near the castle, in my very own house.

LATIMER:

You are going to take me there right away!

FALSTAFF:

You can think that! Ah! What delirium!
My duty keeps me here.

LATIMER: (distractedly)

You must suspect horrors if I am clarified.

FALSTAFF:

I won't go.

LATIMER: (placing his hand on his dagger)

Well, without mercy or pity
I will kill you.

FALSTAFF: (trembling)

I shall follow you, Milord.

(aside)

I'll die of fright.

LATIMER:

This perjury,
This insult.
Yes, I swear it,
You will admit it.
Your persistence
Is an offense.
Without resistance
You will follow me.

FALSTAFF:

But what perjury?
But what insult?
I swear to you
Alas, I'm unaware of it.
What dementia.
There can be no vengeance
For this non-existent offense.

(During this exchange Olivia has appeared in the doorway of the pavilion. Latimer notices her, and the cowardly Falstaff discreetly takes this opportunity to disappear.)

OLIVIA:

Latimer!

LATIMER:

Olivia!

(swiftly hiding the bouquet still held in his hand)

OLIVIA:

You here? At this hour?

LATIMER:

Now that's just what I was about to say to you: you here at

this hour?

OLIVIA:

Latimer, everything is pure, everything is noble in our love except your jealousy, which darkens and troubles it.

LATIMER:

Olivia, I ought to have found you in London tonight. You were not at the rendezvous, and then—But no, I will not insist that you justify yourself. I shall ask nothing of you. Nothing except to hear your voice and to harvest in my heart the feeling of your presence.

OLIVIA:

We must part.

LATIMER:

But—

OLIVIA:

Right away.

LATIMER: (aside)

Why's she sending me away so quickly?

OLIVIA:

Goodbye, Latimer, goodbye!

LATIMER:

One moment, just one.

OLIVIA:

Hurry then.

LATIMER:

Tell me Olivia, that bouquet….

OLIVIA: (aside)

Heavens!

LATIMER:

That bouquet that you received from me this morning. Now that you've worn it for long hours.

OLIVIA:

Well?

LATIMER:

Detach one flower from it, just one, give it to me, and I shall leave. I shall leave happy.

OLIVIA:

That bouquet? I no longer have it. I lost it.

LATIMER:

You lost it?

OLIVIA:

Yes.

LATIMER:

You didn't give it to someone?

OLIVIA:

No.

LATIMER:

You wouldn't also have lost that ring of my mother's that I gave you, on the day, when before God, you swore undivided love to me? You remember, Olivia?

OLIVIA:

Yes. That was the day you swore to me a boundless trust. Have you forgotten it, Latimer?

LATIMER:

But still, that ring?

OLIVIA: (extending her hand)

That ring, here it is! Do you think me unworthy of wearing it, Latimer? Do you want to have it back?

LATIMER:

No! Oh! No! My God! If you knew, Olivia, I ask nothing better than to believe you.

OLIVIA:

Well, yes, my friend, have complete confidence in me. Later, I'll explain to you.

(mysterious music. Olivia listens anxiously)

But leave! Leave! I entreat you.

LATIMER: (after a pause)

Well, yes. I'm leaving.

OLIVIA:

Oh! Thanks! Thanks!

LATIMER: (aside, astonished)

Thanks!

OLIVIA:

And till tomorrow.

LATIMER: (controlling himself)

Till tomorrow!

(aside)

Oh—I intend to know if I've been betrayed.

(Latimer vanishes to the right. Olivia enters the pavilion at the left.)

(Shakespeare appears at the back and comes forward looking around himself distractedly, like a man still absorbed by a remainder of sleep.)

SHAKESPEARE (singing)

Where am I?
Is this an enchantment?

Is this an enchanter's dream?
My God—if it's a dream
Prolong
This momentous joy!
From a Zephyr's breath
What sweet scents.
My mouth happily sucks in
That sweet flowery perfume.
Who then will appear to me
In this fine garden?
Ah! My soul conceives itself to be
The soul of Romeo.
Beneath this azure vault
Come to me, to your creator.
Come, adored Juliet.
Come intoxicate my heart.
Let your presence complete
All this happiness
Make my most beautiful dream
A reality.

(Elizabeth appears in the doorway of the pavilion; she is veiled, she comes forward.)

SHAKESPEARE: (noticing her, and completely delirious)

Why, there she is, great God! It's she!
O my ideal beauty.
Yes, I made you immortal
And you embellish my enchanted eye.

ELIZABETH:

No, I am not Juliet.
Hear me.
Wake up, poet.
Wake up!

SHAKESPEARE:

Who are you?

ELIZABETH:

Me? I am the genius
That disorder exiled from your heart.
And England, and your noble country
Intends to recall its poet to honor.
Obey me, let your soul be prepared.
Hear me.
Poet, awaken from a long sleep.
Wake up!

SHAKESPEARE: (speaking in time with the music)

My genius, my genius. But when it calls me it's with a silent, secret voice, and yours strikes my ear.

ELIZABETH:

That's because your outraged genius has been obliged to separate herself from you and become your judge.

SHAKESPEARE:

No, indeed! That's impossible.
I am the plaything of a dream!
It's intoxication that's disturbing my reason.

ELIZABETH: (with spirit)

William Shakespeare, this hour is a solemn hour for you.

SHAKESPEARE:

But if you are a marvelous apparition, celestial beauty must splendorize your face. Let me see you, let me contemplate you! Or at least let me hear your voice.

ELIZABETH: (stepping back)

Well, listen.

SHAKESPEARE: (ecstatic)

Oh, yes, speak to me!

ELIZABETH:

If I forever abandon you
There'll be no halo about your face.
The mob, instead of crowning you,
Will hold you in shame and disgrace.

SHAKESPEARE:

Me, Shakespeare, shamed and disgraced!

ELIZABETH:

No more thought in your lost soul
Nor wit in your lofty mind.
No, no mausoleum near our kings.
Cursed by God, you will completely die.

SHAKESPEARE: (beside himself)

Ah! I shiver, what a curse.
To avoid this destiny,
What must be done,
O my genius, in this supreme moment?
What must be done? Alas, speak, I shall obey.

ELIZABETH:

From disorder, from unworthy orgies
Let your parting be eternal.
You must respect genius
Which descended from heaven to you.

SHAKESPEARE:

Your will gives me a new being
Yes, I feel it.
The poet, at last, is going to be reborn

In your accent!

ELIZABETH:

For you my wishes
Will mount to heaven;
For you my heart
Wants glory and splendor.

SHAKESPEARE:

Down here, for my life,
For my happiness,
The heart of a friend
Is needed next my heart.

ELIZABETH:

That happiness, you will have on earth.
I promise.
What woman wouldn't be proud
Of your success!

SHAKESPEARE: (carried away)

Ah, my soul is rejuvenated by your voice.
What tenderness in your tone.

(becoming more and more exalted)

No, no, you are not my genius

But better still for me. I conceive
This veil hides a woman, a friend,
With the most seductive allures.

ELIZABETH:

What are you daring to say?
What delirium—?

SHAKESPEARE: (falling to his knees)

O you whose cherished voice
Has such great power o'er my heart,
Illusion of my whole life
I will see you, I want to see you!

ELIZABETH: (aside)

My God! My God! His dear voice
Has such power o'er my heart.
Alas, will it cost me my whole life
To reject such a sweet hope?

SHAKESPEARE:

Your sight is happiness.
Come, bring to my life
This enchanting dream
That comes to intoxicate my heart!
Ah! If you've ravished me!
On me, misfortune! Misfortune!

O you, whose dear voice, etc.

ELIZABETH:

My God! My God! His dear voice, etc.

SHAKESPEARE: (totally intoxicated)

I shall brave all in my delirium

(trying to remove Elizabeth's veil)

ELIZABETH:

Someone's is coming. Misfortune.
It's your death.

(Shakespeare turns to see who's coming. Elizabeth manages to disengage herself. At the same moment, Olivia, appearing at the pavilion door, grabs Elizabeth and hurries her into the pavilion.)

OLIVIA: (aside)

Just heaven!

SHAKESPEARE: (seizing Olivia's hand, taking her for Elizabeth)

Stay, oh, stay longer.

OLIVIA: (turning, trying to flee)

Flee!

SHAKESPEARE:

For you, my heart, my life—

OLIVIA:

Leave!

LATIMER: (entering)

Olivia. It is she. Perfidy!

OLIVIA: (aside)

Latimer. O misfortune!

LATIMER:

Infamy! Infamy!

OLIVIA:

Don't believe it.

LATIMER:

Shut up! Shut up!

OLIVIA:

Mercy, listen to me!
I swear it. My innocence
And my vows.

LATIMER:

They're broken!

(he hurls the bouquet to the ground and tramples it underfoot.)

OLIVIA: (aside)

Oh, heaven. I can hardly breathe.
What to do? I cannot tell him.

SHAKESPEARE: (to Latimer)

Enough, Milord, enough. Jealousy
Is distracting your wits.

LATIMER: (beside himself)

You, the accomplice
Of her felony must fight for your life with me.
But you won't hear this call of honor
For those fine sentiments with which you adorn
The hearts of your heroes,
Why, that's mere poesy.

(disdainfully)

No, no, you won't fight!

SHAKESPEARE: (indignant)

Me! Me! I won't fight!
I shall punish that infamous doubt.

LATIMER:

In that case, follow me!

SHAKESPEARE:

Yes, I am following your steps.

LATIMER:

Come.

SHAKESPEARE:

Right away: I'm following your steps.

OLIVIA: (rushing to stop Latimer, who pushes her away as he leaves. She staggers and falls)

I'm dying.

SHAKESPEARE: (about to follow Latimer, rushes to Olivia)

What do I see! Help! Help!

ELIZABETH: (unveiled, rushing out of the pavilion)

Great God! Olivia! My Olivia!

OLIVIA: (rising up with effort)

Ah, Madame, Latimer! Ruined! I am ruined!

ELIZABETH:

Ruined! Noble girl—

SHAKESPEARE: (to himself as he looks anxiously at Olivia and Elizabeth)

That voice.

ELIZABETH:

Ruined, and for having taken my place.

OLIVIA:

Oh! Be quiet! Be quiet, Majesty.

SHAKESPEARE: (excitedly)

The Queen.

ELIZABETH: (with authority)

Silence!

SHAKESPEARE: (to himself, with exaltation)

It was the Queen.

ELIZABETH: (dragging Elizabeth into the pavilion)

Come, come!

(to Shakespeare before disappearing)

Silence!

LATIMER: (returning, sword in hand)

Well, I'm waiting.
You won't escape my just vengeance here.

SHAKESPEARE:

For her, milord, no offence.
Don't outrage so much innocence.

LATIMER: (raging)

Ah, your cowardly heart hesitates, I see that.
Wretch, you shall fight.

(threatening to hit Shakespeare with the flat of his sword)

SHAKESPEARE: (putting himself on guard)

You insist on it, because of your dementia.
Ah! Before God, you'll answer for it.

(They fight.)

FALSTAFF: (with game wardens running in from all sides)

Ah! Wretches! Cease
To cross swords in a royal castle.

(trying to separate them)

LATIMER: (beating him)

Get back.

SHAKESPEARE: (also beating him)

Leave us alone.

FALSTAFF:

See such audacity!
Why, it's a capital crime.
William, Milord Stop!
Because it's a capital crime.

CHORUS:

Was ever such audacity seen!
Why, it's a capital crime!

(Shakespeare pierces Latimer, who stumbles and falls into the wings)

ALL: (uttering a shout)

Ah!

SHAKESPEARE:

Killed! Execrable crime!
Let's flee! Let's flee!

(Shakespeare runs off like a madman)

CHORUS:

What a shocking crime!

(All rush to where Latimer fell. The curtain falls.)

CURTAIN

ACT III

The Palace of White Hall

Rich reception hall. Gallery in the back. Doors right and left.

ELIZABETH (alone)

Despite these dazzling surroundings,
So many sad, boring days.
To the head that wears the crown
Cares flock to attach themselves.
Love, sweet, intoxicating love
That brings happiness
And tender spirits
Flees from my heart. Ah!
But, if necessary, poor queen
Resist today
The inclination drawing me
To watch over him carefully forever!
My God! Let my soul have
It's sweet, pure passion.

From the height of my grandeur
Let's watch over his happiness!
Come, dreams of glory
Come console my heart.
In history
My name must live with honor.

(to Olivia)

Well, Olivia? Sir John Falstaff?

OLIVIA:

He's going to be here, Madame. I was afraid the would return to his house, and that—

ELIZABETH:

Impossible! I have the key he gave us at the tavern, and besides, since this morning I made him come from Richmond to Whitehall, with the order not to leave this palace.

OLIVIA:

Ah! I'm dying of fear and impatience. How anxious I am to—

ELIZABETH:

…To know whether Latimer is wounded or not.

OLIVIA:

It's true. But what worries me especially is Your Majesty's honor. For, in the end, Shakespeare recognized you, Madame, and he's going to believe you love him.

ELIABETH:

Oh—he must be unaware of that!

OLIVIA: (stupefied)

Eh, what, Madame?

ELIZABETH:

Calm down. If Elizabeth, if a woman is not mistress of her feelings, the Queen must be mistress of her grandeur and her glory!

OLIVIA: (looking to the back left)

Here's Falstaff, Madame.

ELIZABETH: (rapidly to Olivia)

Come on, dear child, courage. The need to act has restored my gayety and my courage. Second me.

FALSTAFF: (appearing in the gallery at the back, speechless, aside)

And to have as yet proved unable to find my two adventuresses! Probably, I was stupid to give them my key. They must have ransacked my house.

USHER: (announcing)

Sir John Falstaff.

ELIZABETH: (seated to the right, whispering to Olivia).

There's nothing about his manner. The duels can't have had fatal consequences. He's such a coward, it would have made him ill, I'm certain of it.

OLIVIA: (whispering)

Oh! What a kindness you are doing me, Madame.

ELIZABETH:

Sir John Falstaff?

FALSTAFF:

Majesty?

ELIZABETH:

Well, come forward, will you!

FALSTAFF:

I was awaiting the order of my sovereign.

ELIZABETH:

I have just that, an order to dictate to you.

FALSTAFF:

To me?

ELIZABETH: (pointing to a table)

Sit there.

FALSTAFF:

I obey.

(going to the table and placing his hat on it.)

ELIZABETH:

And prepare to write.

FALSTAFF:

Yes, Queen.

ELIZABETH:

It's an order that you will execute yourself after having obtained the signature of the High Sheriff.

FALSTAFF:

This is an honor for me.

ELIZABETH:

Are you ready?

FALSTAFF:

I am indeed, Majesty.

ELIZABETH: (dictating)

Our High Sheriff of London, on behalf of the Queen. We order Sir John Falstaff....

FALSTAFF:

I am in favor, that's clear.

ELIZABETH:

…To search for, and to find, in order to hang him….

FALSTAFF:

It's a question of hanging someone with my intervention! I am in the good graces of my sovereign, that's evident.

(aloud, repeating)

So as to hang him.

ELIZABETH: (dictating)

One of the governors of our royal castles, whose name we are unaware of, who doesn't husband the deer of Her Majesty under the pretext Her Majesty cannot count them.

FALSTAFF: (aside, a bit terrified)

The Devil!

ELIZABETH: (dictating)

Who doesn't stint himself either from reserving the choicest meats for himself and only allows the Queen second best quality.

FALSTAFF: (increasingly terrified, aside)

Ah! My God! I see what it is; the two adventuresses from the tavern have denounced me. And there I was, giving them my key—

ELIZABETH: (rising)

So what's wrong with you, Sir John Falstaff?

FALSTAFF: (troubled)

I—Queen—I....

ELIZABETH:

Yes, I understand; you are indignant at the behavior of this unknown governor, you, probity itself

FALSTAFF: (feigning modesty)

Oh!

ELIZABETH:

Fidelity itself.

FALSTAFF:

Oh! Oh!

ELIZABETH:

Precision, even.

FALSTAFF:

Oh! Oh! Oh!

ELIZABETH:

Yes, precision in person, and you are going to give me proof of it by telling us all that took place yesterday, at night, at Richmond park, where you were on guard.

OLIVIA:

Ah! At last!

FALSTAFF:

Oh! If she knew that the park was invaded and that—Why, I'd be ruined.

ELIZABETH: (to Olivia)

You are going to see, my dear, with what clarity and in what scrupulous detail, Sir John Falstaff is going to give us his verbal report.

(The Queen sits to the left in an arm chair which Falstaff has just moved forward for her.)

FALSTAFF: (aside)

Her Majesty's calm reassures me.

ELIZABETH: (to Falstaff)

We are listening to you.

FALSTAFF:

Madame, I am desolated not to have any great thing to report to Your Majesty.

ELIZABETH:

We are not asking for an amplification from you, Sir John, we are asking you for the truth and nothing but the truth.

FALSTAFF:

I'm going to lie. What's needed is nerve.

ELIZABETH:

Sit down, Miss Olivia.

FALSTAFF:

Well, madame, thanks to my active supervision all was perfectly calm last night at Richmond Park.

ELIZABETH:

Ah!

FALSTAFF: (to Elizabeth)

Yes, Majesty.

OLIVIA: (seated to the right)

Ah!

FALSTAFF:

Yes, Miss Olivia.

ELIZABETH:

You saw nothing?

FALSTAFF:

Nothing but moonlight.

ELIZABETH:

Ah!

FALSTAFF:

Yes, Queen.

OLIVIA:

Ah!

FALSTAFF:

Yes, Miss Olivia.

ELIZABETH:

And you didn't hear anything?

FALSTAFF:

Just what is ordinarily heard.

ELIZABETH:

What's that?

FALSTAFF:

The stags troating, the nightingale singing, the breeze blowing, insects buzzing, the foliage shaking.

ELIZABETH:

That's all?

FALSTAFF:

That's all.

ELIZABETH:

Ah!

FALSTAFF:

Yes, Madame.

OLIVIA:

Ah!

FALSTAFF:

Yes, Miss Olivia.

ELIZABETH:

I believe you.

FALSTAFF: (aside)

I am saved.

ELIZABTH:

Still, a trusty person insists they heard wrathful voices—

around midnight.

FALSTAFF: (aside)

Ah, they told her.

(aloud)

That's just what I was going to have the honor of telling Your Majesty.

ELIZABETH:

You see, Olivia, with what minutia—he forgets nothing. Arms were heard clashing!

FALSTAFF: (aside)

Ah! My God!

ELIABETH:

What was that?

FALSTAFF:

Guards quarreling.

ELIZABETH:

No.

FALSTAFF: (looking at Elizabeth)

No?

ELIZABETH:

No.

OLIVIA: (to Falstaff who turns to her)

No.

FALSTAFF: (in the same tone)

No, that is to say, poachers fighting.

ELIZABETH:

No.

FALSTAFF:

No?

ELIZABETH:

No.

OLIVIA: (to Falstaff, who turns to her)

No.

FALSTAFF: (in the same tone as the Queen and Olivia)

No!

ELIZABETH:

You mean two duelists.

FALSTAFF:

That's exactly what I was about to have the honor of—

ELIZABETH:

And you didn't recognize them?

FALSTAFF:

They fled so rapidly when I appeared.

ELIZABETH:

One was named a certain Lord Latimer, the other the poet, Shakespeare. But look, the details, Explain yourself. I wish it.

FALSTAFF: (aside)

The safest thing is to tell everything.

(aloud) Well, Majesty, Let's start at the beginning. I found myself at the Mermaid Tavern when two women, two adventuresses....

ELIZABETH:

Unnecessary. Keep going.

FALSTAFF:

Then I received an order to transport a large package.

ELIZABETH:

Unnecessary again. The story of the duel, nothing else, a faithful account.

FALSTAFF:

Yes, Majesty. Here it is then. Lord Latimer that I thought grievously wounded—

OLIVIA: (excitedly)

Well—

FALSTAFF:

Slipped on the turf as he was raging. Without doing himself the least harm.

OLIVIA: (excitedly)

It is true?

FALSTAFF:

Without the least scratch.

ELIZABETH: (looking at Olivia, brightly)

See how minutely he describes all that—

OLIVIA: (hand on heart)

Yes, oh, yes, Sir John. You narrate very well.

FALSTAFF: (with false modesty)

One of my minor talents.

ELIZABETH: (with great interest)

And the poet?

FALSTAFF:

The great poet, the sublime Shakespeare, my intimate friend....

ELIZABETH: (sharply)

Cut it short!

FALSTAFF: (proudly)

Believing his adversary dead, he fled completely terrified. In his distraction he passed over brambles, thickets and hedges, jumped a wall in the park and landed in the water. Boatmen pulled him out faint and motionless, and took him home. I've just learned he's still asleep.

ELIZABETH: (after manifesting extreme anxiety, sighing slightly)

Ah!

FALSTAFF:

That's the faithful account I have to give, Your Majesty.

ELIZABETH:

Fine, that's fine.

(whispering to Olivia)

Now that we know everything

(pointing to Falstaff)

He must know nothing.

(as Falstaff passes to the right, the Queen as she speaks goes to the table where Falstaff's hat is and places the key in his hat.)

That's very fine, Sir John. You just gave us a fine sample of your imagination, and that's a pleasure, I wanted to obtain for Elizabeth.

OLIVIA:

Yes, Sir John's account did me a lot of good.

ELIZABETH:

But I prefer the first because it has the merit of being true.

FALSTAFF: (aside, disconcerted)

What's that signify?

ELIZABETH:

That, my fine teller of tales, you didn't meet two adventuresses at The Mermaid Tavern. And it's I who tell you so.

FALSTAFF: (nearly speechless)

It's quite possible—

A SUMMER NIGHT'S DREAM * 139

ELIZABETH:

You didn't receive an order from the High Sheriff to transport something or other to Richmond.

FALSTAFF: (exhibiting a paper)

It's strange how one can be deceived. I really thought that this paper—

ELIZABETH: (snatching the paper and tearing it up)

That paper is an error.

FALSTAFF: (speechless)

Evidently.

ELIZABETH:

Lord Latimer and the poet Shakespeare never entered the park. So they couldn't have been dueling as they left.

FALSTAFF: (mechanically)

Not dueling at all.

ELIZABETH:

And here's what happened at Richmond last night, and nothing else. Recall your original memories, Sir John, it's extremely important and quite true. The stags troated.

FALSTAFF:

The nightingale sang.

OLIVIA:

The breeze sighed.

FALSTAFF:

The insect hummed.

ELIZABETH:

And the foliage shivered.

FALSTAFF: (stupefied)

Why, that's exactly what I had the honor of telling Your Majesty.

ELIZABETH:

And exactly what you will tell without addition or deletion to anyone who may question you about it.

FALSTAFF:

Yes, Queen.

ELIZABETH: (taking the writing she dictated to Falstaff)

Otherwise you will share the fate of the unknown governor described herein.

FALSTAFF: (terrified)

I'll be hanged.

ELIZABETH: (sweetly)

Just like him.

FALSTAFF: (aside)

One rope will do for the two of us.

ELIZABETH: (giving him a sign to withdraw)

That's fine.

FALSTAFF: (bowing, aside to himself)

At last, I've got the time to go to my dwelling to see those two women.

(picking his hat up from the table.)

ELIZABETH:

But don't leave the palace. I have orders to give you.

(whispering to Olivia) Now for Shakespeare. And don't say anything yet to Latimer.

(aloud) Follow me, Sir John.

FALSTAFF:

Yes, Majesty.

(aside)

Ah, how wrong I was to give them my key.

(going to put on his hat and finding the key, he stops in stupefaction. Elizabeth and Olivia smile.)

(aside) My key.

ELIZABETH: (leaving)

Well, what's keeping you, Sir John?

FALSTAFF:

I am with you, Queen, I am with you.

(aside) It's sorcery and for twelve hours the devils have been at my heels.

(leaving totally speechless after the Queen)

OLIVIA: (alone, sighing)

Heaven grants my prayers
At last my heart is calmed
About his cherished life.
But, alas, it's a mystery
About which my voice must still be silent.
I will obey this duty.
Yes, even at the price of his tenderness
I will guard the honor
Of my noble mistress,
From all suspicion,
From all insult.
I intend that my Queen be pure.
I will obey this duty.

LATIMER: (entering, with emotion)

Olivia!

OLIVIA:

It's him.

LATIMER: (wishing to withdraw)

Pardon, madame
If once more I offer myself to you eyes,
But before leaving these parts
A final duty calls me.

OLIVIA:

A duty?

LATIMER: (controlling himself)

Yes, I'm coming to ask of you
My mother's ring,
That a dear and faithful spouse
Alone has the right to keep.

OLIVIA: (scornfully)

Can it be?

LATIMER: (getting excited)

Are you worthy of keeping it?
No, no! I am betrayed even by my courage.
And on the rival who outrages me
I have not been able to avenge myself—
But I'll see him again.
Let him tremble; I'll punish him

OLIVIA: (in anguish)

Calm this delirium

(aside)

If only I could tell him.

(aloud)

Trust me!
I've kept my word.

LATIMER:

No, no. You are betraying our childhood friendship,
And the oaths we exchanged.
What could have told me that my presence today
Would come to break such sweet bonds.

OLIVIA: (bitterly)

Ah, as in the time of our infant friendship
Believe, trust, the oaths I took!
I swear by God who knows my innocence
I am worthy of your love as ever.

LATIMER:

Ah! It's in vain that your heart hopes—

OLIVIA:

With a final hope
I swear
On this ring, your mother's ring.

LATIMER:

That's too much! At least let this sacred pledge
Be still respected by your hands.

OLIVIA: (sorrowfully)

This last outrage
Has broken my heart.

(offering him the ring)

Take back this pledge
This pledge of joy

(he takes it after hesitating momentarily)

But this ring that I've just given back—
Regretting your jealous suspicions
Soon, perhaps, at my knees
You shall pray me to take back.

LATIMER:

Forever, I forswear
My credulity.
There's been too much perjury
Disloyalty.

OLIVIA:

Ah, my soul is pure
Of disloyalty.
Of perjury,
Of infidelity, forever.

USHER: (enters, announcing)

William Shakespeare.

LATIMER: (threatening)

Ah!

OLIVIA: (with terror)

Great God!

ELIZABETH: (who has appeared, to usher)

In a moment.

(the usher returns to the gallery at the back)

OLIVIA: (whispering excitedly to Elizabeth while pointing to Latimer)

Madame, prevent a new meeting.

LATIMER: (bowing)

Majesty!

(starting to withdraw)

ELIZABETH:

Milord, don't leave this palace.

(reaction by Latimer)

Go! And attend my orders.

(exit bowing by the right. Olivia, at a gesture from the Queen leaves by the left.)

ELIZABETH: (to usher)

Introduce William Shakespeare.

(the usher signals Shakespeare to enter)

(struggling visibly against an emotion that she succeeds in dominating)

That's well, William Shakespeare! You haven't been slow in accepting the invitation I sent you.

SHAKESPEARE: (smiling respectfully and discreetly)

Can you doubt my eagerness, Madame?

ELIZABETH:

I profited by a circumstance that assembled all those who are most distinguished in my realm, to request you near our person.

SHAKESPEARE:

I thank Your Majesty.

ELIZABETH:

I wanted to have a ceremony for it the first time I saw you.

SHAKESPEARE: (aside, smiling)

O, the first! Actually, the second.

(aloud)

The first time, Madame?

ELIZABETH: (smiling, completely mistress of herself)

I am not thinking of the theatre which is your home, I am speaking of the first time at my home.

SHAKESPEARE: (with a mysterious smile, tempered with respect)

Then the park at Richmond no longer belongs to Your Majesty?

ELIZABETH: (slightly emotional)

It still belongs to me.

SHAKESPEARE:

Well, last night....

ELIZABETH: (very moved)

Last night—

SHAKESPEARE:

It seemed to me....

ELIZABETH:

You were at Richmond?

SHAKESPEARE:

If I'm not mistaken....

A Summer Night's Dream * 151

ELIZABETH:

And you saw me there?

SHAKESPEARE:

That's the way it seemed to me.

ELIZABETH: (after a smile of feigned astonishment)

Now that's your poetic imagination.
It takes illusion for reality.

SHAKESPEARE:

Madame, it's true. At first I thought it was an illusion, the apparition of a fairy, a genie. But soon I felt it was something more, that it was a woman, that it was—

ELIZABETH, (interrupting him, with emotion)

William Shakespeare, probably that's a scene from a comedy you are preparing—for our ceremony. I would like it because you are a great poet.

SHAKESPEARE: (with a touch of irony)

It's true, Madame, I am only a poet, and some ambitious woman I'd never imagined, stretched audacity to the point of—

(bowing)

ELIZABETH: (aside)

Oh! If he knew—

SHAKESPEARE: (pulling himself together)

But yet, that night which recently unfolded, that night which was madness for me to hope for, and a crime to seek, that night which must henceforth preside over my life, that impossible night, if you like.— Someone created it for me, someone wanted it to be mine. And it is not an illusion, it's a reality.

ELIZABETH:

A reality?

SHAKESPEARE:

That had three witnesses, Madame.

ELIZABETH:

Who are they?

SHAKESPEARE:

Your Majesty, first of all. Then myself, and later a lady of honor whose memory will, perhaps be more accurate than mine.

ELIZABETH:

You think?

SHAKESPEARE:

I'm sure of it.

ELIZABETH:

And her name is?

SHAKESPEARE:

Miss Olivia.

ELIZABETH: (rings a bell. To a Lady of Honor who appears)

Miss Olivia!

LADY OF HONOR:

Here she is, Madame.

(withdrawing)

ELIZABETH: (to Olivia, who enters)

My darling Olivia, William Shakespeare, whom I present to you wants to address a question to you about an event which appears to interest him greatly.

SHAKESPEARE:

Oh! More than my life!

ELIZABETH:

I invite you to reply to him.

SHAKESPEARE:

Miss Olivia, last night you were at Richmond, weren't you?

OLIVIA: (feigning astonishment)

At Richmond?

SHAKESPEARE:

Yes, in the park, with Her Majesty?

OLIVIA: (to Elizabeth)

I was in the Park at Richmond with Your Majesty?

ELIZABETH:

That's what William is asking you. Search your memory.

SHAKESPEARE:

Yes. You were there, right?

OLIVIA:

I was in London with the Queen.

SHAKESPEARE:

And you didn't go to Richmond?

OLIVIA:

No.

SHAKESPEARE:

Eh! What, you must have forgotten the violent scene that took place there, as a result of which you fainted?

OLIVIA:

I swooned? Me?

SHAKESPEARE:

Yes, when a bouquet was thrown at your feet.

OLIVIA:

A bouquet was thrown at my feet.

SHAKESPEARE:

By Lord Latimer.

OLIVIA:

By Latimer?

SHAKESPEARE:

What? You don't even recall his abrupt return, his fury, his delirium, and that fatal battle?

OLIVIA: (at a sign from the Queen)

No.

ELIZABETH: (excitedly)

After all these replies what you were thinking can only be a mistake.

SHAKESPEARE:

A mistake!

ELIZABETH:

Unless it's merely a fiction on your part.

SHAKESPEARE:

A fiction!

ELIZABETH:

Well, in that case, necessarily, it must only be a dream.

SHAKESPEARE:

A dream!

OLIVIA:

Yes, yes. It must be a dream.

ELIZABETH: (singing)

It's a dream.
Merely a dream
That's over
Right now.
The delirium

That it inspires
Can seduce
Only for a moment,
A single moment!
It's charm comes to you from too far away
To banish it. Ah! What torture!
And as for me, I am the Queen.
Often, I say as I sigh.
It's a dream
Merely a dream
That's over
Right now.
The delirium
That it inspires
Can seduce
Only for a moment.
It's a poetic dream
That changed into reality
Would become a comedy.
The dream of a summer night.
It's a dream, etc.

(Repeat first eight lines)

(Elizabeth leaves followed by Olivia, after giving Shakespeare a look of tender compassion.)

SHAKESPEARE: (alone, after a moment of stupefaction)

The dream of a summer night! But can the impression a dream makes have as much power, as many consequences as lucidity? Did I dream I was in the Mermaid Tavern? That they were giving a party for me? That I met a masked lady there that....

(silence)

...That as a consequence it came about—? How did I leave the tavern? How did I find myself in Richmond Park? There's a strange lacuna here! But Still, I didn't dream that in that enchanted park a genie appeared to me! That genie was a woman! That woman is a queen!

(searching)

And that—they! Ah, Latimer arrived unexpectedly! He took me for his rival. We crossed swords! I struck him mortally! Falstaff arrived with his game wardens! I fled. I leaped over the park wall.

(searching)

What happened after that? I felt a frozen shivering. And then? And then—nothing, futility! How was I carried home? I don't remember. There's more, too....

(troubled, agitated)

Eh! What do I care what I've forgotten? Does what I remember have the least reality? It's useless for the Queen to say she regrets her imprudence. That's all. But Miss Olivia whose lover I struck down? How's she doing?

(completely disoriented)

My God! My God! Will no one come to tell me— My conscience is my conviction. "William Shakespeare, you didn't dream all this."

(Falstaff appears at the rear)

FALSTAFF (aside, dreaming without seeing Shakespeare)

Hanged! Hanged twice! That's too much by half. What am I saying by half....

SHAKESPEARE: (noticing Falstaff and rushing to him)

Ah! My good, Sir John. My dear Falstaff! My savior!

FALSTAFF: (stupefied)

Eh!

SHAKESPEARE:

My friend, my excellent friend.

FALSTAFF: (proudly)

Yes, it's I, Sir John here—I have the honor to be the friend of the famous Shakespeare, of this sublime intelligence—

SHAKESPEARE: (smiling in self-pity)

So sublime that a mere nothing troubles him. Tell me, Falstaff, perchance you dream at times?

FALSTAFF:

Often, of my loves, about my meals—I cannot escape it.

SHAKESPEARE:

And your dreams impress you like reality?

FALSTAFF:

Absolutely.

SHAKESPEARE:

So that after waking the illusion persists?

FALSTAFF:

Completely.

SHAKESPEARE:

To the degree that reality is not more shocking?

FALSTAFF:

To the degree, dear friend, that no later than last week, having dreamed of an amorous escapade in which I received from a badly brought up husband a volley of kicks in the—I'll skip the word. And in which I sprained my ankle while leaping from a balcony. The next morning when I woke, I actually limped while doing my duty at Richmond.

SHAKESPEARE:

Richmond. Isn't there a marvelous park at Richmond?

FALSTAFF:

A fairy park.

SHAKESPEARE:

And you're the one who guards it, isn't that true?

FALSTAFF:

Yes, dear friend.

SHAKESPEARE:

Were you there last night?

FALSTAFF:

Yes, I was there.

SHAKESPEARE: (aside)

Ah!

(joyfully)

And could you tell me what took place there?

FALSTAFF: (forgetting himself)

Lots of things happened!

(trembling)

SHAKESPEARE: (aside)

By Jove, I was sure I wasn't deceiving myself.

(aloud) Lots of things happened?

FALSTAFF: (thinking better of it, in a natural tone)

My God, extremely ordinary things.

SHAKESPEARE:

Ah! But what? What took place?

FALSTAFF:

The stags troated, the nightingale sang, the wind sighed, the insects hummed, and the foliage shook.

(aside)

And so did I.

SHAKESPEARE: (stupefied)

And nothing more?

FALSTAFF:

Nothing more.

SHAKESPEARE:

You didn't see Olivia?

FALSTAFF: (excitedly, with a feeling of terror)

I didn't see her.

SHAKESPEARE:

And the Queen?

FALSTAFF:

Not at all.

SHAKESPEARE:

And Latimer?

FALSTAFF:

No more!

SHAKESPEARE:

And William Shakespeare?

FALSTAFF:

Least of all!

SHAKESPEARE: (explosively)

Why, no, that's impossible! And if I dreamed all the rest of it, one detail of this strange night which comes to my mind I didn't dream. I killed Latimer!

(At this moment Latimer crosses the stage at the back in conversation with some gentlemen of the court.)

FALSTAFF:

Latimer? Behold.

SHAKESPEARE: (seeing Latimer pass.)

Great God! Why, then am I certain of mine own existence?

(in despair)

Ah! I feel reason is abandoning me, and all that remains for me is to die.

FALSTAFF: (looking at him frightened)

Die—him—die! Ah, let's run to warn the Queen.

(Falstaff hurries out by the back right.)

SHAKESPEARE: (collapsing into a chair overwhelmed)

(singing)

A dream! What! It was a dream?
Waking comes to ravish me of everything!
Banishing this intoxicating lie.
Then, better far to die!
I was near her, she was queen
I hoped for a sweet future.
Glory, love—all vain shadows.

Got to die!

(Shakespeare rises. Latimer reappears hand on the hilt of his sword, and takes a step towards Shakespeare. The Queen appears at the side door. Latimer quickly conceals himself behind a door.)

ELIZABETH:

Shakespeare, whither are you going? You are not leaving this palace at the moment the ceremony is about to begin?

SHAKESPEARE:

I ask Your Majesty's permission to withdraw.

ELIABETH:

Stay, Shakespeare!

SHAKESPEARE: (wanting to leave)

I cannot.

ELIZABETH:

I insist on it! I've been told everything.

SHAKESPEARE:

Well, yes, I have to die.

ELIZABETH:

Die? And why die?

SHAKESPEARE:

To avenge you, madame, for the insult I gave Your Majesty here.

ELIZABETH:

And if I've forgotten it?

SHAKESPEARE:

It's something I have to remember.

ELIZABETH:

And suppose I order you to live?

SHAKESPEARE:

You will be ordering me to do the impossible.

ELIZABETH:

To live for the glory of England, to make my reign illustrious!

SHAKESPEARE:

No, Madame, every drop of poetry is drained out of me! For one single thing is true about what I thought had taken place last night.

ELIZABETH:

What's that?

SHAKESPEARE:

That my genius has left me. Left me forever.

ELIZABETH:

Forever? How do you know that, William?

SHAKESPEARE:

Everything is over, I feel it, and if the poet no longer sings, he must die.

ELIZABETH:

And if your genius returned?

SHAKESPEARE:

It won't return!

ELIZABETH:

It will return, I tell you, and the proof is—

SHAKESPEARE: (distracted)

The proof is I am mad.

ELIZABETH:

The proof is that the genie of last night is here, right in front of you!

SHAKESPEARE:

You, Madame!

ELIZABETH: (excitedly)

Let that be a secret to all except for the fiancé of noble Olivia.

(Agitation behind the door that conceals Latimer.)

SHAKESPEARE: (intoxicated)

Why in that case, I didn't dream!

ELIZABETH:

No!

SHAKESPEARE: (exalted)

Ah!

ELIZABETH:

No, you weren't dreaming, if you said to yourself, "The brilliant crown worn so nobly by Dante and Tasso, I William Shakespeare have let fall, and the hand of a Queen has stopped to place it back on my head."

SHAKESPEARE: (with passionate gratitude)

Oh, yes. I owe you Madame—

ELIZABETH:

But, William, you must understand that last night's interview at Richmond can only be for you the audience of a—protectress....

(Shakespeare acquiesces, sadly)

...of a friend.

SHAKESPEARE: (joyous)

Of a friend!

ELIZABETH: (emotionally, but with dignity)

Yes, of a friend, but one who is at the same time a Queen.

(The Court enters. Latimer as the Queen receives the homage of courtiers who have entered, raises the curtain where he'd been hiding and rushes to the feet of Olivia.)

LATIMER:

Pity! Pity! Ah, I was too cruel!
Olivia, I implore you!
Take back this ring. Mercy!

OLIVIA:

Not yet.

(raising Latimer)

You shall give it me at the altar.

ELIZABETH: (to the Lords and courtiers)

To you Milord, to you, Lordships,
To all of you who, for the nation
Wish glory and splendor

(making Shakespeare come forward)

I present a noble genius!

(All the lords bow)

CHORUS:

Glory to Shakespeare!

SHAKESPEARE: (with intoxication)

Ah! So many honors for me!

ELIZABETH:

Come on, William, let my voice encourage you!
Come on, my poet, to work.
Make the kings and warriors of your land
Live again in your writings.

FALSTAFF: (to Shakespeare)

Make heroes in a comedy
Of the merry companions who dog your steps everywhere,
Your shade, if you like, shall not kill.

SHAKESPEARE:

Yes, Falstaff, in my works you shall live.

FALSTAFF: (to himself)

Meanwhile, we actually shall live hereabouts.

CHORUS:

Glory to our Queen!
Noble sovereign!

ELIZABETH: (dashingly to Shakespeare)

God wishes it, God ordains it.
Yes, your renown radiates
Over your native land.
Your glory, poet,
Is my conquest, too.
For it reflects
On my royal head band.

(Shakespeare kneels before the Queen who gives him her hand to kiss)

CHORUS:

God will it, God ordains it.
Yes, your renown radiates
Over your native land!
And the poet's glory
Is her conquest, too.
For it reflects
On her royal head band!

(The Curtain lowers)

CURTAIN